Wet Playtime Games

Rainy day resources for calmer classrooms
By Jenny Mosley & Helen Sonnet
pictures by Mark Cripps

Positive Press

Published in 2005 by: Positive Press Ltd, 28A Gloucester Road, Trowbridge, Wiltshire BA14 0AA
Telephone: 01225 719204 Fax: 01225 712187 E-mail: positivepress@jennymosley.co.uk Website: www.circle-time.co.uk

Text © Jenny Mosley and Helen Sonnet, illustrations by Mark Cripps
ISBN 190-4866-182

Printed by: HERON PRESS, 19-24 White Hays North, West Wilts Trading Estate, Westbury, Wiltshire BA13 4JT

How to use this book

Rain happens. In fact, it happens all too often. If you want to beat the gloom and dispiriting fretfulness it can bring, you need to have everything ready before the clouds loom and spoil your day. Here are a few tips that will help.

Be ready!

Teachers need to agree what the children can be allowed to play with in the class during wet playtimes. Draw up a list, laminate it and display it on the wall. In this way, all the supervisors know exactly where it is and can't be drawn into endless energy-sapping arguments with the children. Find a shelf or a box that you can designate as your wet playtime container and make sure that it contains everything you need for a stress-free wet playtime: scrap paper, crayons, scissors, white boards, felt-tip pens, board games, comics, jigsaw puzzles etc.

Rain supervisors

Give an allocated 'wet playtime helper' responsibility for the maintenance of the wet playtime container. It will be their job to keep your box/shelf nice and tidy and ready for action. Checking that the jigsaws are complete and the felt-tip pens are in working order can be their wet playtime activity, so choose a few children who like to keep things organised.

Involve parents

Send a letter home and ask for contributions to your wet playtime container. Ask for jigsaw puzzles, board games and comics and you'll be surprised how many families will contribute. A surprising number of children adore colouring books and will sit together chatting and colouring for an entire wet playtime. You can buy these books very cheaply in 'pound' shops. Ask your school PTA for a small contribution to set you up with some each term.

Never let a craze go stale

Even wet playtimes have their crazes – colouring one month, chess games the next – but interest will eventually wear thin so you need to be ready with your next craze before boredom sets in. Keep something hidden in the back of the stock cupboard so that you can pull it out at a moment's notice. You could, for instance, hide all of the jigsaw puzzles until everyone has forgotten that they ever existed and then, hey presto, you can pull them out as the next craze.

Use the curriculum

There is always something in the curriculum that really captures children's imagination. Make a note of sure-fire interest generators when you are doing your planning – 3D shapes, map skills, hieroglyphics, different kinds of poetry writing – and have some materials and worksheets ready to give out during wet playtimes.

Don't forget the old favourites

Noughts and crosses, battleships, cat's cradles, consequences, letter strings, atlas games, town/country/river, first letter/last letter, puppet theatres, weaving cards, sewing, finger rhymes and charades – all of these are fully-absorbing, quiet, sit-down activities and children love them.

Duplicate short play-scripts

If you come across some short play-scripts, it is a good idea to duplicate enough copies for each character to have a script. Keep these in a box or drawer and allow children to organise themselves and read them through during wet playtimes. If your older children are talented, they may be able to provide scripts for younger classes and will have the life-enhancing knowledge that their work is being used and enjoyed.

Wet Playtime Games

Every member of the school community feels a sense of gloom when the morning sky turns grey. Raindrops spatter down on a playground that should be resounding with the carefree exuberance of happy children enjoying a time of healthy activity. Everyone knows that children need this time to blow away the cobwebs so that they can return to the classroom refreshed and eager to learn. A rainy-day-shut-indoors feeling makes the whole school restless and edgy and many afternoon lessons begin less happily than they should. Rain is a fact of life but we wish it wouldn't happen at lunchtime!

Wet playtimes don't need to be draining and they don't need to spoil the rest of everyone's day. But they do need to be managed and planned for, and structured so that they can be a productive and positive time for the whole school. Every school needs to have coping strategies in place. They need a set of resources to draw upon and a selection of games and activities that are designed to ensure that wet middays have the qualities of a bright sunny lunchtime even if the outdoors is wet and forbidding.

This book is full of lively and exciting games that will delight all children. All of the activities are designed to stimulate a spirit of co-operation and healthy social interaction, with something to suit every child. For those who like to exercise their minds, there are memory games and activities that require children to pit their wits against an opponent. There are more physical games for those children who need to let off steam and release tensions in a happy, friendly way.

There are fun games of chance and activities for creative children who love to involve themselves in art and drama.

Your children will love to dip into the book time and time again to enjoy the enchanting illustrations and choose a new activity. Staff can join in with group activities and enjoy the positive involvement as a welcome change from supervising fractious cooped-up children.

Like all our Learning through Action books, the ideas and games can be used not just by the adults (in this case the lunchtime supervisors) but also by the older children helping younger children. In many of our Golden Schools, we have children who apply and are interviewed for the role of playground helper. They wear yellow caps out in the playground when they are working in the zoned area, but they also wear them at wet playtimes. Two helpers are assigned to different classes at wet playtime, so under the eye of the mid-day supervisor they can use this book with the younger children. In this way both the older and the younger child will have their self-esteem enhanced.

So, build on the good practice that already exists in your school and use this range of simple but effective ideas to make rainy days seem shorter and brighter!

Helen Sonnet

Jenny Mosley
(Member of the QCA PE and
School Sports (PESS) Steering Committee)

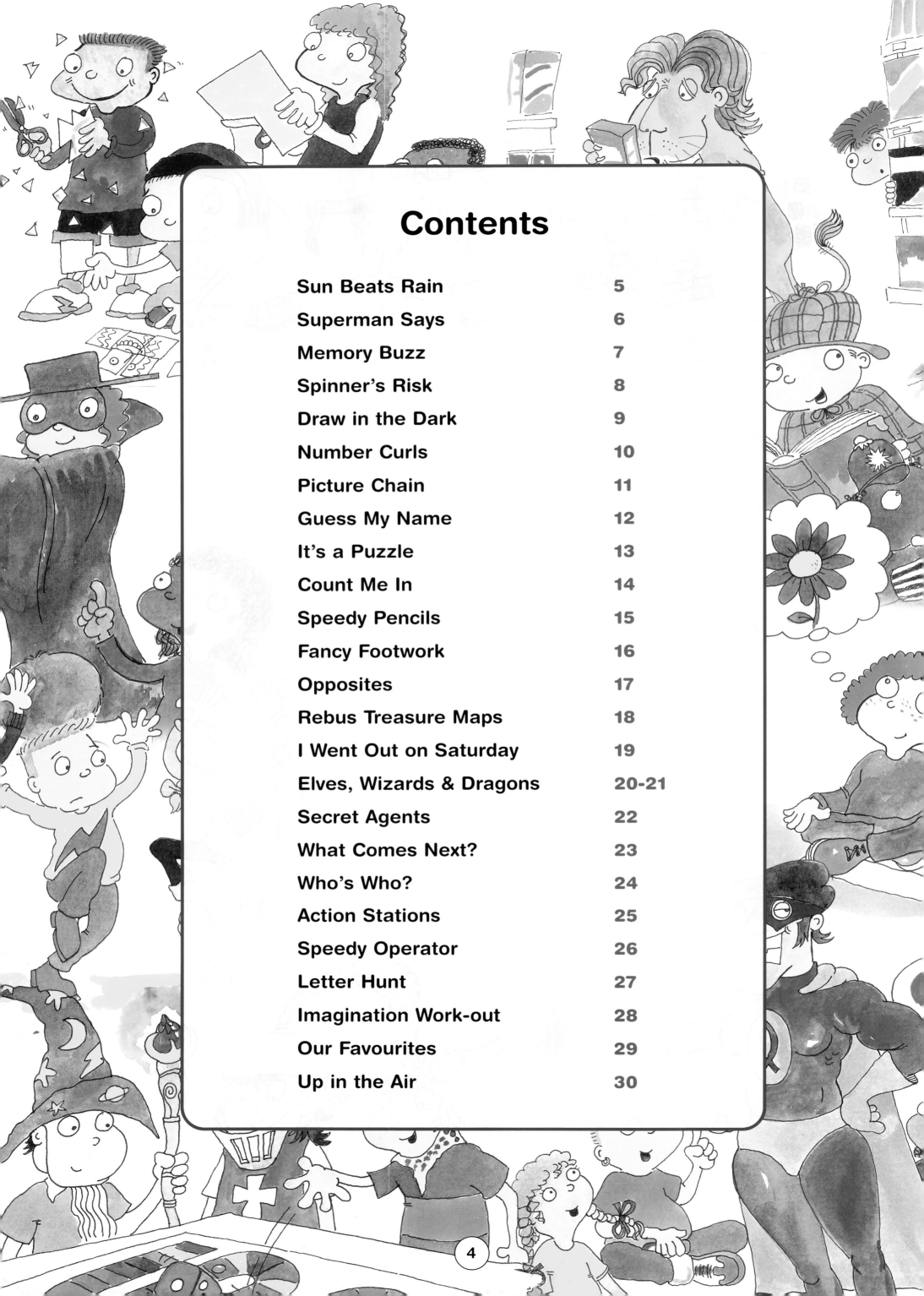

Contents

Sun Beats Rain	5
Superman Says	6
Memory Buzz	7
Spinner's Risk	8
Draw in the Dark	9
Number Curls	10
Picture Chain	11
Guess My Name	12
It's a Puzzle	13
Count Me In	14
Speedy Pencils	15
Fancy Footwork	16
Opposites	17
Rebus Treasure Maps	18
I Went Out on Saturday	19
Elves, Wizards & Dragons	20-21
Secret Agents	22
What Comes Next?	23
Who's Who?	24
Action Stations	25
Speedy Operator	26
Letter Hunt	27
Imagination Work-out	28
Our Favourites	29
Up in the Air	30

Sun Beats Rain

BEFORE YOU BEGIN...

This is a game for pairs. Photocopy the symbols on page 31 onto card, cut them out and laminate them. You will need two sets of weather symbols for each pair.

Shuffle the cards and place them face down.

Both you and your partner choose a card (sun, rain, frost, cloud, wind). Keep them hidden.

On the count of three, reveal your cards.

The power of each card is as follows:

Sun dries rain, sun melts frost.
Rain warms frost, rain shrinks cloud.
Frost chills wind, frost freezes cloud.
Cloud hides sun, cloud dulls wind.
Wind blows rain, wind cools sun.

The winner scores a point.

Continue to play with different cards until one of you has scored ten points.

HELPFUL HINTS

- The children will learn the status of the symbols quite quickly if you run through them several times together, chanting them as a verse.
- Hold tournaments with winners playing each other until there is a class champion.

Superman Says

Stand in a circle. Shuffle the cards and place them face down.

Choose someone to pick up the top card, turn it over and read out the named category, eg colours.

Say the following chant together:

Superman said the other day, 'How many colours can you say?'

Take turns around the circle to say a different colour.
Anyone who repeats a word or hesitates is out of the game.

When someone is out, the next person in the circle takes the next category card and begins the action again.

Continue until you have a winner.

BEFORE YOU BEGIN...

This is a game for three or more players. You will need a set of cards, each labelled with a different category such as football teams, colours or farm animals – anything you wish. There are photocopiable examples on page 31 which can be laminated.

HELPFUL HINTS

- For younger children, make large, clear flashcards and help them to read each category.
- Relate categories to your current curricular topics such as 3D shapes, kings and queens and so on.

Memory Buzz

BEFORE YOU BEGIN...

This is a game for three or more players.

Sit in a circle. Someone begins the game by saying:

'I went on holiday and packed...' (name the item).

The next player repeats the sentence and adds another item to the list.

Continue around the circle, with each player repeating all the items that have previously been named, before adding a new one.

Play until the list becomes too long for a player to remember everything. Then begin again!

HELPFUL HINTS

Try other memory games such as 'I went to the supermarket and bought...' or 'I went to the zoo and saw...'

Spinner's Risk

First, make your spinner. Place the hexagon shape on the card and draw round it.

BEFORE YOU BEGIN...

This is a game for pairs. You will need card, hexagon shapes from your maths equipment, pencils, rulers and scissors.

Then, carefully cut out the card hexagon.

Divide the hexagon into six equal parts by joining the opposite corners with a straight line.

HELPFUL HINTS

Write a different task in each section.

• Discuss possible tasks before you begin, to give everyone an idea of what is needed: something to challenge or make you laugh! Younger children may need help to scribe their tasks on the spinner.

• Examples of tasks might include: 'Sing a song', 'Stand on one leg and recite a poem', 'Say the alphabet backwards' and 'Say ten animals without stopping'.

Insert a pencil through the centre of the hexagon to make a spinner.

Take turns to twist the spinner and perform the task.

Draw in the Dark

BEFORE YOU BEGIN...

This is a game for two or more players. You will need paper and pencils.

Sit on the floor.

Decide on a simple picture that you are going to draw – it might be a house, a tree, a cat – anything you like!

Put the paper on the floor behind your back.

Now try to draw the picture on the paper that is behind you. You must not look at it while you are drawing!

Share your drawing. Can the others guess what you have drawn?

HELPFUL HINTS

Large sheets of strong paper are best for this activity. Make sure that the children are not sitting on flooring that can be damaged by stray pencil marks!

Number Curls

Draw a curling line of squares across your paper, big enough to contain words and counters.

Number each square. Write 'start' at the beginning and 'finish' at the end.

Think of a theme for your number curl – spies, wizards, the Olympics, a day at the shops – and decorate the background to show your theme.

Think of suitable signs of good luck that will enable players to move forward more quickly. For example, 'You find a magic star. Move on two squares'. Add some reasons for moving backwards, such as 'You meet a ghost. Miss a go'.

Spend a few wet playtimes making your games, then find some dice and counters and spend a few more rainy days playing them!

Picture Chain

This is a game for individuals, but players can take part in this activity together. You will need paper, pencils, scissors and colouring pens.

Fold your paper like a concertina.

Draw a figure onto the folded paper, making sure that the hands of your figure overlap both edges of the folded paper.

Carefully cut around the figure, but don't cut around the hands.

Open out your paper to make a chain of figures and colour them in.

For children who need help or support, photocopy the templates from page 32 onto card and cut out.

Guess My Name

BEFORE YOU BEGIN...

Together, make a list of animals. Write each name onto a piece of card.

This game is for two or more players. You will need pieces of card and pencils.

Shuffle the cards and place them face down.

One player takes the first card. The other players take turns to ask questions that require a yes or no answer, until someone guesses the animal's identity.

The game continues with players taking turns to pick up a card.

HELPFUL HINTS

- For younger children, add a picture of the animal alongside its name. Photocopy the examples from page 32 onto card, cut out, colour and laminate them.

- Older children may like to make lists of cartoon characters or contemporary celebrities or topic-related historical figures.

It's a Puzzle

Find a picture that you like in a magazine and glue it onto card.

When the glue is dry, turn the card over and draw jigsaw shapes or cutting lines on the back.

Cut the picture into pieces using your cutting lines. (Don't make the pieces too small.)

Give the cut-out pieces to a friend. Can they put the jigsaw back together to make the picture?

BEFORE YOU BEGIN...

This game can be played by individuals or in pairs. You will need old magazines, glue, large pieces of card and scissors.

HELPFUL HINTS

- For younger children draw a grid on the back of the picture so that the squares can be cut out easily.
- Children can make puzzles using pictures they have drawn themselves.

Count me in

Stand in a circle.

Give everyone a number from 1 to 20 (or more than one number if your group has less than 20 children).

Practise counting quickly up to 20 around the circle.

Now count in twos (only the children with even numbers should speak).

Now count in odd numbers to 20; multiples of four; and multiples of five (again, only the children who have the relevant numbers should speak).

The object of the game is to see how quickly everyone can count in these different ways without making a mistake.

BEFORE YOU BEGIN...

This is a game for groups of four to twenty players.

HELPFUL HINTS

- Ask the children to say their numbers a few times before they start to make sure they know them. It may help to give each child the relevant number tile(s) to aid their memory.
- If young children can't manage multiples of four and five, they can count back from 20 to 1.

Speedy Pencils

BEFORE YOU BEGIN...

This is a game for two or more players. You will need pencils and paper.

Think of something that everyone will be able to draw.

You must be able to explain the details of your picture. Here are some ideas: a house with four windows, a door and a chimney; a flower with a stem, two leaves and eight petals; a cat with a stripy tail, long whiskers and black paws.

On the word **'GO'** all players draw the picture, including all the details.

The first person to draw the picture as it was described wins a point.

HELPFUL HINTS

Make a bank of idea cards featuring items that the children can draw. Print them onto card and laminate them, or use the examples from page 33.

15

Fancy Footwork

BEFORE YOU BEGIN...

This is a game for two or more players.

Face one another, or stand in a circle if there are more than two players, and say the following chant:

Fancy footwork 1, 2, 3,
Watch this very carefully –
Can you do the same as me?

One child performs a sequence of movements with their feet. This could include a jump, three hops on the right foot and a turn on the left foot.

The other players now try to copy the sequence exactly.
Everyone can have a turn at thinking up a sequence of movements.

The challenge is to copy each sequence without making a mistake as they get more complicated.

HELPFUL HINTS

If you are playing with a group, players who make a mistake once must stay out of the next sequence. If they make two mistakes in a round, then they are out of the game. The winner is the child still standing when everyone else is out.

Opposites

BEFORE YOU BEGIN...

This game is for two or more players.

Sit facing each other (in pairs) or in a circle (as a group). Someone should begin by saying a describing word, such as hot.

Everyone must clap twice. The next person in the circle now says the opposite word (eg **cold**). Again, everyone claps twice.

The third player (if you are in a group) must now say another describing word (such as **tall**). Everyone claps twice, and the fourth player now says the opposite, (**short**).

Continue in this way with two claps in between each person speaking. The object of the game is to see how fast you can get things moving.

HELPFUL HINTS

You don't need to use opposites every time you play this game – you can use associations. Someone says the first word and then the next child says a word that comes into their head. Continue until everyone has had a turn.

Rebus Treasure Maps

Work out as many rebus word-pictures as you can and collect them in a class book. Remember that you can use letters for parts of the words.

Draw a map of a treasure island with lots of features such as hidden caves, secret coves and ruined towers. Decide on some locations for the hidden treasure.

Explain the locations using rebus sentences. Share your maps with other pairs or groups. Can they work out where the treasure is hidden?

BEFORE YOU BEGIN...

This is a game for pairs or small groups. A rebus is a word puzzle in which the syllables of words are represented by pictures of things that sound the same. For example, parts of '2 bee or knot 2 bee' can be written in picture form.

HELPFUL HINTS

Try to start a craze by interesting a single group of eager children in this activity and leave them to show it to other groups. The craze should catch on quite soon! Many children will build complex stories around a treasure map. Store the maps safely and the activity might keep them happy for weeks with little adult input required.

I went out on Saturday

BEFORE YOU BEGIN...

This game is played best with six or more players.

Stand in a circle.

Someone begins the game by saying:

I went out on Saturday.

The rest of the group then responds with:

Tell me, tell me, where did you go?

The first player chooses another child in the circle who has to decide where you went on Saturday (a football match, the zoo, a shop, the beach).

The rest of the group now asks:

Tell me, tell me, what did you see?

The first player now names as many people, objects and animals that can be thought of that might have been seen at the venue.

When you have run out of ideas, start the action again with different players.

HELPFUL HINTS

- Add another dimension to this game by allowing children to see if they can slip in something impossible – a lion at the shops, for instance. They earn a point if nobody notices.

- Extend the range of the game by using other senses. For example, *What did you hear?*

19

Elves, Wizards & Dragons

BEFORE YOU BEGIN...

This is a game for two players. You will need photocopied grids of the game from page 34. Use the counters if you wish.

Sit facing your partner. Stand a large, open book between the two of you so that you cannot see each other's grid.

Write the following letters on the large grid, on any squares of your choice:

G for gnome, **W** for wizard, **E** for elves (three times), **D** for dragon and **K** for King.

The object of the game is to capture all of your opponent's characters.

Take turns to call out a grid reference (**A5, C2, G1** and so on.)

Each time you call a grid reference, mark it on your grid to record which grid references you have already said.

Every time a grid reference is called, your partner tells you if he has anything on that square. Use a different colour pen or pencil to cross off empty squares and add in characters as you find them.

HELPFUL HINTS

- Teach this game to older children and encourage them to organise an 'Elves, Wizards and Dragons' tournament among themselves. They can teach the game to younger children and organise a tournament for them too.
- Make certificates and badges to award in each tournament.

When your partner finds one of your characters, cross it off on your grid so you know what you have lost.

There are some additional rules to remember:

The gnome has two lives. When your partner captures your gnome, you can write it in again in another blank square.

Your wizard has the power to save one elf (unless he is captured before he has the opportunity). You can move this elf to a new square.

If your dragon is hit, it captures one of your opponent's elves before it dies. Your partner must cross out an elf and you can make a note of it on your tally. They must also tell you which square it is in.

If you capture your opponent's King, you get two extra goes.

The winner is the first player to capture all of their opponent's characters.

Secret Agents

Here is a secret code:

This is a game for two players. You will need paper and pencils.

Write a secret message for your friend to decode.

Write letters to another class using secret codes. Give the other class the letters and a key and ask them to send replies.

Make flap books with questions in code on the front of each flap and the answer hidden underneath.

Why not try to make up a secret code of your own?

You can photocopy this page so that several children can refer to the code at once.

What Comes Next?

BEFORE YOU BEGIN...

This is a game for two players. You will need an ordinary pack of playing cards.

Shuffle the cards and place the pack face down on the floor or table.

Take turns to guess whether the next card will be black or red.

If you are right, keep the card. If you are wrong, give the card to your partner.

When all the cards are gone from the pack, count up your cards to see who has the most.

Play the game again, but this time guess whether the cards will be numbers or pictures.

HELPFUL HINTS

If younger children find a pack of cards too big, you can split it into two halves as long as you remember to put one red suit and one black suit in each half pack.

Who's Who?

BEFORE YOU BEGIN...

This game is more fun with four or more players.

Choose someone to lead the game. They must think of someone to pretend to be, keeping their identity secret. This could be a real person or a character in a book or film.

The rest of the players ask questions to find the identity of the secret person. Examples of questions might include: Is the person male or female? Is she real or a character in a book? Have we seen him on television? Does he have black hair?

The leader can only answer yes or no but may remind the group of the information that they have built up.

HELPFUL HINTS

- Speed things up by allowing the leader to begin the game by giving one clue or the initials of the secret person.
- Younger children can play a simpler form of the game by identifying people who are in the room with them.

Action Stations

Make sure everyone is seated in a circle.

Shuffle the activity slips and place them face down in the centre of the circle.

Take turns to take a slip and mime the activity from the centre of the circle. The first player to guess the activity has the next turn.

When a player has guessed an activity twice, they can make up an activity of their own for everyone to guess.

BEFORE YOU BEGIN...

This game is more fun with eight or more players. You will need a selection of activities written onto slips of paper. Some examples are: washing the floor, hanging out the washing, cleaning the car, putting the shopping away, making the bed. Alternatively, photocopy the examples on p33 onto card.

HELPFUL HINTS

- For younger children, use pictures stuck on to card.

- Older children can add adverbs – quickly, slowly etc – so that they must perform the activity in the way that the adverb describes.

25

Speedy Operator

BEFORE YOU BEGIN...

This game is for larger groups of players (ten or more) and may need the supervision of a teacher or midday supervisor.

Stand in a circle.

Someone begins by showing the next two children on the left a sequence of hand actions. For example, clap three times, touch both shoulders, touch your head, then fold your arms.

On the command 'GO', the two children copy the sequence. The last one to complete the actions is out.

The child who is left must show a new sequence to the next two children on their left.

Continue the game until only two players are left in the circle. The last child to complete a sequence must show a new sequence for the pair to perform.

The winner is the child who completes the final sequence in the fastest time.

HELPFUL HINTS

This game can be played sitting on the carpet. One child sits at the front of the group and demonstrates a sequence of actions that are copied by the group. Then, another child is chosen to be leader – this might be the fastest or slowest child in the previous game.

Letter Hunt

BEFORE YOU BEGIN...

You will find alphabet tiles, a dictionary and an atlas helpful for this game.

Choose some letter strings and write them on card, such as 'ing', 'ar', 'tion' etc.

Use your wet playtime to hunt for as many words as possible that contain the letter string you have been given.

Use a dictionary to find new words that contain the letter string. Copy out the word and definition.

Another way to organise the hunt is to take a letter of the alphabet and an atlas. You can search for rivers that begin with 'A' or towns that begin with 'W'. The possibilities are endless. Don't cheat by using the index!

HELPFUL HINTS

Have a reward ready for the most productive group. This can be a privilege such as the right to go to lunch at the head of the line or five minutes free time at the end of the day.

Imagination Work-out

BEFORE YOU BEGIN...

Gather a few items that will help you to get thinking about the categories that are listed on this page. Display the items on a table to help ideas to start flowing. Add some categories of your own.

Choose a category from the following list. Give everyone some scrap paper and the task of dreaming up ten things that will fit a particular setting or situation.

10 things that are smaller than a mouse.

10 things that you might find in a king's dungeon.

10 things that taste horrible.

10 things that a giant might keep in his kitchen.

10 things that use water.

10 things that are red.

HELPFUL HINTS

- Use your current curriculum for ideas: 10 things that you would find inside a pyramid or that are made from particular materials, for example.
- Ask younger children for smaller numbers of items.

Our Favourites

Everyone sits in a circle.

Start the action by rolling the ball across the circle to anyone you choose. Ask a question, such as 'What's your favourite dinner?'

The player with the softball should answer the question. Then, they roll the ball to someone else and ask either the same or a different 'favourite' question.

Continue in this way, making sure everyone has a turn at asking and answering a question.

BEFORE YOU BEGIN...

If you have the luxury of extra space at lunchtime or can use the hall, then this game is ideal. It is suitable for two or more children, and you will need one softball.

HELPFUL HINTS

Ideas for 'favourite' categories are: football club, sweet, cartoon character, pet, TV programme, colour, pop star.

Up in the Air

Everyone stands in a circle holding a balloon.

On the command 'GO', throw the balloons into the air.

The object of the game is to keep all the balloons in the air. Anyone can hit a balloon that is near to them even if it is someone else's balloon.

Once a balloon touches the floor, all the balloons have to be retrieved and the game begins again.

BEFORE YOU BEGIN...

This is a game that is great for allowing players to let off steam when you have more space available. It is suitable for two or more players. You will need an inflated balloon for each player.

HELPFUL HINTS

- Ask someone to time the action with a stopwatch to find the longest period the balloons can be kept in the air. Try to beat the record.
- Keep a balloon pump to hand for speedy inflation.

Sun Beats Rain Symbol Cards (p5)

Superman Says Category Cards (p6)

colours	animals	cars	flowers	football teams
shapes	trees	farm animals	clothes	sports

Picture Chain Templates (p11)

Guess My Name (p12)

cat	dog	elephant	horse
pig	cow	hippo	monkey

Speedy Pencils Subjects (p15)

A spotty dog with droopy ears and a big bushy tail.	A bird with a round body, a short neck, a hooked beak and very long legs.	A flower with four pointed spotty petals and two oval leaves.
A wizard with a long beard, pointed hat and a long cloak decorated with stars.	A garden with a small tree, three flowers, two birds and a big sun in the sky.	A sandcastle with two towers, a round door, two windows and a stripy flag on top.

Actions Stations (p25)

Washing a car.	Brushing a dog.	Planting a tree.
Playing an instrument.	Washing some clothes.	Building a wall.

Elves, Wizards & Dragons Counters (p20-21)

Elves, Wizards & Dragons Grid (p20-21)

	A	B	C	D	E	F	G
1							
2							
3							
4							
5							
6							
7							

Notes

Other titles in the Learning Through Action series

Skipping Games

By Jenny Mosley and Helen Sonnet, illustrated by Mark Cripps

The skipping activities in this book are designed to proceed from the simple to truly impressive displays of magnificent agility. They have catchy chants that bring rhythm, humour, exercise, accomplishment and companionship to your playground, making it a happy place full of those who spend their free time doing something that has been enjoyed since rope was invented. You will find both traditional and modern chants in this book. You could even create some of your own.

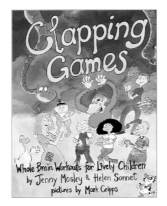

Clapping Games

By Jenny Mosley and Helen Sonnet, illustrated by Mark Cripps

This first collection of clapping games includes old favourites and brand new rhymes. With colourful illustrations and beautiful details, the games in this large format, full-colour book develop listening skills, head and hand coordination, memory and language skills in a fun and entertaining format. Includes CD.

More Clapping Games

By Jenny Mosley and Helen Sonnet, illustrated by Mark Cripps

Building on the success of the first book, this collection (in black and white A4 format) expands the repertoire with 30 new clapping games which will appeal to older as well as younger children. Includes a DVD, demonstrating the games as performed by KS1 and KS2 children.

Playground Games

By Jenny Mosley and Helen Sonnet, illustrated by Mark Cripps

Here is a rich store of the games and activities we had access to as children: playground games that teach children about teamwork, leader and follower skills and, most importantly, how to have a good time as part of collaborative group imagination.

To order a catalogue, please contact:

Positive Press Ltd.
28A Gloucester Rd
Trowbridge, Wiltshire
BA14 0AA
Tel: 01225 767157
Fax: 01225 755631
E-mail: circletime@jennymosley.co.uk
Website: www.circle-time.co.uk

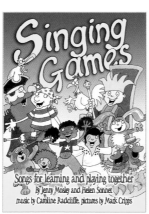

Singing Games

By Jenny Mosley and Helen Sonnet, illustrated by Mark Cripps

Songs for children to learn together and sing together with an interactive twist that brings fun and energy to the classroom. The skills needed for singing together carry with them the skills of memorisation, co-operation and concentration. The simple lyrics in this collection make the songs easier to remember, with lots of rhyme and repetition. Some of the songs in this book are old favourites with familiar tunes while others are new - but all are engaging and easy to follow. A simple melody line is included for each song if you want to play along. Includes CD.